MEDITATIONS
WITH MASTERS OF THE
AXIAL AGE

Charles Pacello

Print ISBN: 978-1-54397-401-0

eBook ISBN: 978-1-54397-402-7

TABLE OF CONTENTS

PREFACE

The path to spiritual enlightenment is not an easy one. Our world today desperately needs a profound spiritual resurgence of the deep truths, the mystical and philosophical truths that underlie every major religious tradition. They are the universal laws which govern the conduct of the soul and its relationship to existence. The soul is an instrument of truth. Its nature is to seek that which is true, that which is holy, and that which is pure. The soul cannot tell a lie. However, people can, and often do, when their conscience – that still small voice which whispers in our hearts to 'do this', or 'don't do this' – is snuffed out by the rampant unbridled temptations, delusions, violence, greediness, lusts, and deceptions plaguing our societies. We are constantly bombarded, on a daily basis, with lies, distortions, and betrayals of trust originating from our political leaders, our religious institutions, our governments, our corporations, our business community, our multifaceted diverse media, and from those dearest to us, our families and friends. As a consequence of our loss of conscience and faith in humanity, doing the right thing and living in integrity with ourselves and others, is no longer the way we normally operate in our lives, and tragically, fear is the predominant emotion coursing through our veins. We don't trust each other. This absence of trust is having a deleterious effect on our emotional and mental wellbeing. Anxiety is on the rise, depression is reaching epidemic proportions, the suicide rate continues to climb, and we have become the most drugged and medicated population in the history of civilization! What has become of us?

Our modern society has lost its moral compass. The advances in technology, engineering, and the sciences have created a world of instantaneous messaging, YouTube videos, Facebook, Live radio/TV programming, Uber, Lyft, Twitter rants by public officials, Instagram, and WhatsApp. People from all over the globe can download information, news, reports, and uplifting memes just by pressing a button on the computer or IPhone. Public shaming based on bite-size videos clips have become all-too-common. Innocent individuals' lives are being threatened, even destroyed by the vicious attacks made by a sometimes misinformed, but none the less a voyeuristic, angry society. Banking can be done simultaneously while engaging a friend or spouse in conversation while at our work or leisure. Our children now spend hours every day playing video games with their friends, each one sitting at home on their laptops talking to one another on headphones as they do battle in virtual war zones. And of course, there are the larger challenges we must face. Our nation's economic inequality continues to widen, our natural resources are being depleted, climate change is happening before our eyes, while first priority of our governments is to continue to invest, develop, and maintain their nuclear arsenals, and we seem to be asleep to the dark, hazardous trajectory this places the whole of humanity on. Why would we want to leave to our children a world threatened by nuclear annihilation? What will wake us up before we reach the point of no return? When will we, as a people, stand up and say, 'No More!' to the dark forces lined up against us which we all had a hand in creating?

A tragic consequence of the materialism, consumerism, and the technologically-driven mind-set of contemporary culture is the contempt, disdain, and complete disregard for the wisdom, knowledge, and the understanding of human nature handed down to us by the wise masters of the ancient world. The masters may not have had the technology we have today however, they were more intimately connected to the mechanisms that governed the soul – its laws, virtues, vices, and the ways in which a human being could be corrupted, or redeemed, from a life that had veered off 'The Way'. An individual's soul was of primary concern to these ancient masters – they believed that what a person thought, spoke, and did had profound consequences in their earthly life, but more importantly, in the afterlife, when the totality of our deeds were weighed and evaluated by Him/Her who created us. There are no secrets in Heaven. Everything is known. Every word uttered remembered and recorded. These ancient masters believed we were held accountable to the Heavens, and that what we did in this life mattered. It mattered to treat people well – the way you want to be treated – and not to cause harm to another human being. To the masters, the spiritual realm was more real than the physical world. No one was responsible for your soul but you, and you must walk the path; no one could do it for you. They could show you the way, but you still had to take the journey. You were in charge of your soul. Thus, for one who did evil, there were consequences, and for those who did good, blessings. Life would test you – to see which choices you would make when confronted with lies, deceptions, cravings, and temptations. If you had not cultivated a strong soul, a sturdy spine, inevitably you would fail your tests, and the mark on your soul would be with you into eternity. (Ironically, it's in the failing of some of the tests that helps us to grow stronger, as we learn from our mistakes, work to atone for our errors, and make amends). In the monotheistic traditions of Christianity and Islam, both later-day flowerings of the original Axial Age in Israel, a soul faced eternal damnation in hell, while in the eastern traditions of Hinduism and Buddhism, a soul would be placed on the wheel of suffering, continuously reincarnating on the earth until the karmic consequences of his or her bad choices, sins, had finally been dissolved and appeased. Regardless of which spiritual tradition you come from, one thing seems to be a universal truth from all civilizations throughout time: what we do in life matters, in this world and in the next. So why are we no longer learning from the great masters of the past? Why do we no longer study their works to ascertain the wisdom, the knowledge their scholarship offers us? Are we too arrogant to believe they have anything of value to teach us?

There is much the ancient masters knew that we have collectively forgotten or ignored, and if remembered, studied, and practiced, could benefit our world immensely. A vast majority of the sages, philosophers, prophets, and spiritual masters of the epic period in human history called the Axial Age (900 BCE – 200 BCE) were not as concerned with what you believed, your theology, as much as they were focused upon how you behaved. The spiritual life was not just about rituals, sacrifices, and ceremonies; but of more significance, was how to live an ethical and moral life. The masters dedicated their intellectual, emotional, and spiritual capacities to understand and examine the qualities of the soul – kindness, compassion, courage, temperance, justice, love, trust, hope, and faith – and developed systems that would allow their disciples and others to follow a certain, defined disciplined path which would ultimately lead them to making personal contact with the Divine. Despite all of our material advancements, we have never exceeded the profound spiritual insights made during the Axial Age. And in times of social, political, or moral crisis, we have often returned to these great luminaries of the past for guidance. Hence, I believe, we must do the same thing in our times.

It was important for aspirants of any of these spiritual paths to reflect on the teachings of the master, meditate on the deeper significance and symbolic meaning, and pray to God or their gods for guidance on how to incorporate this wisdom into their own lives. Each supplicant or student would ask themselves relevant questions to dig deeper into the teaching in order to personify what could often be abstract, paradoxical, and difficult to comprehend. If the student could make it his or her own, then this spiritual insight would take root in their soul, and as a happy consequence, they would begin to practice these teachings in their ordinary lives. The soul has to be trained in the ways of the soul; otherwise the ego will take over.

It was this understanding which planted the inspiration for this book – let each reader spend a little time with a few of the great masters of the Axial Age. Let them sit down with Socrates, the Greek playwrights, Ezekiel, Lao Tzu, the mystics of 'The Upanishads', and the Buddha. In this hectic world of ours, where life seems to be moving at an ever faster pace, a few moments with one or two of the great teachers could be all the difference in helping us to make meaning of our lives, to remember what is really important, and to guide us on how to live life well.

The book is broken down into four parts, each representing the region where the Axial Age (900 BCE – 200 BCE) was taking shape: Greece, Israel, China, and India. In each section, a brief history is provided, based largely on the brilliant book by Karen Armstrong, *The Great Transformation: The Beginning of Our Religious Traditions*, a work I am deeply indebted to and which in large part inspired the writing of this book. A description follows of the master teacher and his teachings, and concludes with a meditation on that particular subject. I recommend sitting in a quiet place, reading the meditation, reflecting on its deeper meaning, and once read, close your eyes for at least 5 minutes as you contemplate the lesson. Afterwards, there are 4 or 5 questions for you to answer on your own time, in your words, what these teachings mean to you and their significance. I encourage you to answer them in depth, to the best of your ability. As in anything, the more you put into it, the more you will gain from these personal reflections. When satisfied, move onto the next master and follow the same process. By the time you finish the book, my hope is you will have a deep, personal, and passionate intimate connection to your soul, unlike anything you've experienced before. If nothing else, you will certainly come to a renewed awareness of the profound mystery of who you really are.

Health, Love, and Blessings.

GREECE

SOCRATES: THE IMPORTANCE OF 'KNOWING THYSELF'

We are looking at the religious and philosophical traditions that were created during the Axial Age, from approximately 900 BCE to roughly around 200 BCE. The striking similarities each of the four regions' sages, philosophers, and spiritual masters came to is astonishing, as if something was in the air inspiring them to arrive at virtually the same conclusions. The developments of Confucianism and Taoism in China; Hinduism and Buddhism in India; monotheism in Israel; and philosophical rationalism in Greece can all be traced to this enormously critical moment of spiritual revolution and evolution. All four regions' spiritual organization was rooted in violence, fear, and pain. These religious traditions would all agree and insist on not denying our suffering. They would discover that, in actuality, suffering was a prerequisite to enlightenment.

My primary resource that inspired me to create these meditations is Karen Armstrong's book, *The Great Transformation: The Beginning of Our Religious Traditions*, a magnificent achievement in clearly elucidating the historical, cultural, societal, anthropological, and religious movements which led to the great religions in our world today. I refer often to her work throughout this booklet, and encourage the reader to invest some time and effort to read it. Not often do we get in such lucid prose a chance to understand what drove these luminaries to radically shift their emotional, psychological, philosophical, and spiritual ideas away from the violence, war, and trauma of their times towards an ethos of love, compassion, and 'doing unto others what we would want done to us'. If we all would take the opportunity to reflect on the ideas presented in Karen's book, and return to the source of all these sundry religious traditions and the deep truths, insights, and understandings they worked tiringly to pioneer, our world will experience another great transformation. It is my intention for these meditations to contribute in a small way to the awakening of others to the truth that lives in them through the teachings of six of the principal figures of this Axial Age; to push their consciousness beyond the limitations of themselves and the world we have constructed and connect them to the transcendent dimension available to us all within the core of our being. For every individual who devotes his or herself to the lessons in this booklet, I believe you will find something so exquisitely beautiful in the silent stillness of your being that these mediations guide you to, you won't be able to view the world through the same lenses again. My hope is you will be changed as a consequence. If each of us does our part to reach the radiant sun that pulses within our human heart, not only will our consciousness expand, but there will also be an overall collective shift in consciousness towards the heart. This is the goal, intention, and inspiration behind this booklet.

We begin with Greece. The Greeks would experience their Axial Age not so much in its religious context, as they held onto the ancient pantheon of Greek Gods and Goddesses well into the first few centuries of the Common Era, but theirs would be more of a political, scientific, and philosophical transformation. Perhaps the greatest, wisest, and most renowned philosopher to come down to us from the ancient Greeks is Socrates. He was the son of a stone-cutter. An ugly man who had a paunch, snub nose, and protruding lips, Socrates would walk around Athens talking with anybody who was interested in a better understanding of themselves. He believed this was his mission. Socrates didn't charge money for his services, and yet, he always had around him a group of disciples who revered and adored him.

"His purpose was not to impart information, but to deconstruct people's preconceptions and make them realize that in fact they knew nothing at all" (Armstrong, 2006, p. 306). He engaged in dialectic dialogue. This was Socrates' method of exposing false beliefs and untruths, in order to elicit truth, and it was an exhausting affair. Many of his interlocutors would storm off angrily and in confusion because Socrates had shown them how little they actually knew. He had an uncanny ability to move his students through the questioning and answering of a particular idea, analyzing and discovering its flaws and inconsistencies. As a consequence of this intellectual battle to find the deeper meaning of things, those who would engage with him would soon learn and appreciate "the creative profundity of human ignorance" (Armstrong, 2006, p. 307). For Socrates, there was nothing greater for a human being to do than to do work on his soul. By asking these deep questions about life, if we were lucky, we might arrive at some profound truth that would affect how we behaved in the world; however, we could only achieve this if we were willing to interrogate our assumptions.

Socrates saw philosophy differently than many of his contemporaries like the Sophist Protagoras. Philosophy wasn't about conceptual, abstract theories on how the universe was formed; it was about learning how to live well. When we sought to understand what courage, justice, prudence, temperance, and friendship was for us, what it meant to us, we would start to embody this understanding in our lives and work towards making it a reality. If our understanding of these virtues was self-serving or lacked depth, we would live superficial lives and be at the mercy of our baser instincts. A clearer comprehension of the values of the soul could direct our energies and efforts towards the highest good. This was how we cultivated the best in us, in others, and was of supreme benefit for our souls. Socrates took pride in knowing he knew nothing. That it was humankind's failure to examine themselves and their ideas, beliefs, and assumptions that caused so much suffering. If we would recognize our ignorance, we would be able to arrive at intimations that would lead us to how to live and behave well at all times. If we failed to do this, if we did not examine ourselves, we would live empty, shallow lives. As Socrates explained, "The life that is unexamined is not worth living" (Armstrong, 2006, p. 309).

When we failed to think deeply about meaning – the meaning of terms like goodness, honor, love, virtue – we betrayed our soul, or "psyche" as the Greeks called it. To Socrates, "The cultivation of the soul was the most important human task, far more important than the achievement of worldly success" (Armstrong, 2006, p. 309). Our soul is the seat of our conscience. It gives us a sense of ethics and moral responsibility. Socrates described a voice which told him what not to do, which prevented him from hurting someone or betraying himself (Tick, 2005, p.18). This quality of soul was strengthened by choosing good actions and weakened by doing bad. Socrates insisted the only path to happiness was not to retaliate or render evil for evil. We must do all that we can to restrain ourselves no matter what was done or how much we had suffered. It was the Greek example of the Golden Rule, which we will see show up again and again during the Axial Age.

'KNOW THYSELF'

'Know Thyself' was written on the forecourt of the Temple of Apollo at Delphi. It is a command from the god for the highest form of knowledge, the knowledge of the Self. The Self lives within each of us. This quest is the most difficult of tasks, for we are asked to slough off our ideas, beliefs, conceptions, opinions, and perceptions of who we think we are as the world defines us, and through inquiry, discover who and what we truly are at our most essential being. This idea has been woven through the course of history, from ancient times to the modern day. To 'know thyself' is the greatest mystery of all mysteries, and it can take a lifetime to uncover the true nature of our identity. As you do the meditation, keep this in mind that this quest to know thyself is a joyful discovery, that all wisdom begins with wonder; and let us have the humility of Socrates when he says "I do not think that I know what I do not know" (Plato, 1989, p. 8).

'KNOW THYSELF' MEDITATION

Let us turn our attention inward for self-introspection and reflection. 'Know Thyself'. What does this mean to you? Contemplate this maxim for a moment. 'Know Thyself'. Know Thyself. Are you a body? For all appearances, the answer is yes. When you look in the mirror, what you see is a body. But are you a body or, do you have a body? Is there something more? Consider this – your body is made up of 50 trillion cells!...all with their own unique intelligence. The cells receive information, process food, and discard what has been digested. If we look even more closely, at the subatomic level, we find each cell composed of millions of atoms, and when we investigate the atom, what do we discover? 99.99% of you is space! Matter is only .001% of the atom. So what are you? Who are you?

Are you your emotions? Emotions come and they go. Sometimes you're happy, joyful, and content. Other times, angry, depressed, and fearful. Emotions color our lives and give it texture, depth, and aliveness – but is that who we are? Know Thyself. Am I my emotions? Are my emotions reliable enough for me to say 'that is me' – or is there something more, something deeper...

If our emotions and feelings are unreliable, and we are look-ing for something constant, unchangeable, immutable – then what else is there? What is the truth of who we are? Maybe we're our thoughts. But have you ever noticed how our thoughts are like the trains at a train station? They seem to come from nowhere and head off into nowhere – that is, unless we jump on the train and let it take us where it wants to go. Notice too, how we can have con-tradicting thoughts – one moment we think one thing, and we're sure of it – and the next moment we think the opposite, and we're sure of that. Surely we're not our thoughts. Is there something beyond thought? Where do our thoughts come from? If you're not your thoughts, who are you?

If you're not a body, not your emotions, not your feelings, not your thoughts, and not your beliefs – because beliefs are thoughts which we have agreed upon as being appropriate for us and how we choose to perceive the world – then what's left? Consciousness. Consciousness allows us to be aware that we exist. And what gives us the awareness of being conscious? Know Thyself. Know Thyself.

Feel this mystery of who you really are welling up inside of you. The light of awareness that brings you the gift of consciousness is the greatest miracle of all miracles. Feel this light burning deep inside of you. Know Thyself.

There are no words that can carry you beyond this point but only the profoundness of silence. Let us now, as we draw ever closer to the truth of who you are, sit in reverential silence as we come to know our true selves, and let us do this for 5 long, slow breaths.

And on your last breath, as we close out this theme on 'Knowing Thyself', there's a quote by Carl Jung I want to leave you with. "Who looks outside, dreams. Who looks inside, awakens" (http://www.brainyquote.com/quotes/quotes/c/carljung132738.html). Awaken to the truth of who and what you are. Gently, come back into the room, and when you are ready, gently open your eyes.

WORKBOOK QUESTIONS ON SOCRATES AND 'KNOW THYSELF'

What does it mean to you to 'know thyself'?

Why is this valuable to you? Do you see the importance of it? Why or why not?

What does courage mean to you? Justice? Prudence? Temperance? These were considered the four cardinal virtues by the Greeks, are they relevant to cultivate in your life? Why?

What does it mean to 'cultivate your soul'? When answering this question, define what soul means for you.

GREEK TRAGEDY AND THE PURPOSE OF CATHARSIS

Greek tragedy is one of the great contributions of this period. It characterized the spirit of the Axial Age, this pivotal time in the spiritual evolution of humanity, which lasted for the Greeks from approximately 900 BCE to 200 BCE. The vision advanced by the poets and philosophers was so radical for its time, it changed human history forever. Aristotle thought tragedy should be the centerpiece of education in a democracy (Shay, 1994, p. 193); that it had a necessary function to keep the people and the city or society healthy. He believed tragedy helped to educate people about the emotions, how to appropriately handle them, and by evoking pity and fear on the stage, the audience would be able to purge their own toxic feelings and emotions. The ritual re-enactment of a story, where the sufferings of a tragic character unfolded before the audience, would induce, in the end, a feeling of compassion. Feelings of empathy were a necessary condition to create the possibility for harmony between different factions within the community. Tragedy had the power to "transform our deepest fears into something pure, transcendent, and even pleasurable" (Armstrong, 2006, p. 392). It was a means of draining the society through a process called 'catharsis', which was a "cleansing", a deep purification of the soul awakened through the emotional body by grief. Catharsis allowed potentially dangerous and toxic emotions to be released, refined, and purified in both the individual and the society.

The Greeks emerged from a 400 year dark age around 900 BCE. Over time, they would develop and achieve a vision of civilization of incomparable brilliance, an idea of the perfection of humanity that continues to influence our Western world today. Philosophy, law, democracy, art, architecture, and theater are just a few of the contributions we inherited from the Greeks. Despite their enormous achievements, they never lost sight and connection to the tragedies of life that plagued every human being. They understood that life sometimes required one to suffer, that pain and suffering were inextricably linked to this life, and therefore, we must learn how to survive, endure, and get through. "They experienced the sacred in catastrophe, when life was turned inexplicably upside down, in the breaking of taboos, and when the boundaries that kept society and individuals sane were torn asunder" (Armstrong, 2006, p. 62). Wars, violence, and other unnatural deeds brought about these disasters, and if we didn't purge ourselves of that which had wounded us, we and our families would be contaminated by this pollution until it was eliminated. The Greeks called this contagious power *miasma*, and they believed it had an independent life of its own (Armstrong, 2006, p. 64). They identified this dark, chthonic power as the Erinyes (in Roman mythology they are known as the Furies), and they were frightening harpies that would assail, torment, and pursue the wrongdoer. If the wrongdoer remained unpunished, or did not seek ways to make amends and atone for his errors, this *miasma* would affect and contaminate the whole family with more sorrows, traumas, and catastrophe. This inevitably would get passed down the generations until the *miasma* unleashed had been dispersed.

The Greeks understood it was not possible to experience the fullness of life's ecstasy unless you had also experienced loss.

Tragedy helped to bring this understanding to the ritual of theater, where people gathered in ceremony to confront and face their gravest fears and terrors, and experience catharsis. Purged of the pollution contaminating their souls, they learned through their suffering, that it was possible to come out safely on the other side.

Tragedy developed out of the mysteries of Dionysus, the suffering god who went wandering Greece after being driven mad by his stepmother Hera. For three days, the citizens of the polis would assemble in the theater to listen to the choral recitation of the myths. Eventually, these choruses singing evolved into the full-scale drama of Greek tragedy we know today, characterized by tragic plots, flawed characters, and the heroic struggle to overcome epic challenges. Tragedy was a treasured institution. It served as a communal meditation, during which time the audience came to watch and weep. Suffering was an inescapable fact of life and the Greeks put this on stage. "The Greeks firmly believed that the sharing of grief and tears created a valuable bond between people" (Armstrong, 2006, p. 269). Sworn enemies could discover their common humanity. Tears had the power to clear out the grief of their poisonous hatred. Feeling they were not alone in their sufferings, recognizing that all mortals suffer, helped to bridge differences, find common ground, and lay the groundwork for harmony, justice, and peace. "Catharsis was achieved by the experience of sympathy and compassion, because the ability to *feel with* the other was crucial, essential to the tragic experience" (Armstrong, 2006, p. 270).

When we can embrace our sufferings, give ourselves permission to grieve over the tragedies that have happened in our lives, and in the lives of others, the cathartic experience of this emotional, psychological, physical, and spiritual purification keeps our hearts alive. I'm reminded of a favorite quote I hold dear written by the Greek tragic playwright Aeschylus. He wrote: "He who learns must suffer. And even in our sleep pain that cannot forget falls drop by drop upon the heart, and in our own despair, against our will, comes wisdom to us by the awful grace of God" (http://www.brainyquote.com/quotes/quotes/a/aeschylus148591.html).

My question to all of you before we move ahead to the meditation is this: what if you looked at every tear, drop by drop, as wisdom from your pain?

MEDITATING ON CATHARSIS

To be cleansed of suffering, we must grieve, and we must learn. I want you to remember you are in a safe place. Nothing can harm you. The Light that surrounds you, envelopes you, that has cleansed every cell of your being, protects you now. You are safe.

Catharsis. What does that mean to you? What suffering are you holding onto that would melt away with the healing tears of grief? Be gentle with yourself. Choose something that you know in your heart it is time to let go of. You already know what it is. Let go of the hurt, the anger, the pain connected to this situation, be it a person, an event, or something you may have done. Beneath all those toxic emotions polluting your system, is grief. The inevitable losses we have that are part and parcel of this life. Grieve the loss – whether it's a person, a place, a home, a way of life, or perhaps, your own innocence – give yourself permission to grieve. Be gentle and kind with yourself. Grieving over our losses, regardless of what it may be, keeps our hearts alive. Catharsis...this deep puri-fication...this emptying out of all that is poisonous to the health of your mind, heart, body, and soul is the goal. Let the tears flow. Let them flow freely. Remember, God is here. He will wipe away all your tears.

Let us learn and grow from our sorrow. And let us learn from others as well. Gently now, turn your attention away from your-self, and let us feel and empathize with someone else's suffer-ing. Choose an individual trapped in a war torn country; imagine you as a refugee; a Holocaust survivor; a homeless person on the streets. See their life. Imagine what it is like to walk in their shoes. Feel the pain, the sorrow, the horror of their lives – remember, be gentle with yourself. Allow yourself to feel without getting carried away. Let this person's suffering awaken within you compassion, empathy, and love. See them as yourselves. With the same hopes and dreams and longing for a safe, peaceful, joyous life. Catharsis awakens us to feel the life of another – it refines, strengthens, and purifies our emotions to be able to see ourselves through our dif-ficult times and to bring more love and compassion in the world. Breathe. Breathe. Allow the grief you may be experiencing right now to open your heart. Let's open our hearts and embrace the suf-fering of humankind that we all may accept it, honor it, recognize it in our awareness, and then, turn it into something good.

It's time now to release the suffering you have experienced and watched others experience, and deliver it to a higher power. There's a basket in front of you. Imagine now, placing all of this suffering, pain, misery, sorrow, and violence into this basket. Make sure to put it all in there. Hold onto none of it. Before you now, stands an emissary from God – perhaps its Christ, or Buddha, or Lao Tzu; one of the archangels Michael or Raphael; maybe it's the Virgin Mary, or Quan Yin, or another face of the divine feminine – whoever it is, let it be the right emissary for you. They are here to take your sufferings, to take your pains away. The catharsis you've experienced has purged, cleansed, and purified you of all this suffering. See how kindly and lovingly the face of God looks at you. You hand over the basket. The face of God gladly takes the basket from you. You have given your sufferings to a higher power. "I will carry this for you now. You are free of this burden. Go in peace," this being says. Your heart lifts, fills with joy, as this emissary of God takes your sorrows and sufferings and dissolves into the Light. You feel lighter and free. Gratitude swells in your heart.

Let us breathe now 5 breaths in silence in this space of gratitude for the blessings we have received.

On your last breath, as we close out this theme on catharsis, there's a prayer I would like to leave you with:

God grant me the serenity to accept the things I cannot change,

the courage to change the things I can,

and the wisdom to know the difference.

Gently now, come back into the room, and when you are ready, open your eyes.

WORKBOOK QUESTIONS ON GREEK TRAGEDY AND CATHARSIS

Do you share the same beliefs as the Greeks do about tragedy that we can experience sympathy and compassion for another's suffering when we are able to *feel with* the other? Why or why not?

Have you ever experienced a cathartic moment when watching a theater performance or movie? What was it like?

Do you think a modern version of Greek tragedy has a place in our society? Do you think Aristotle was right when he thought it should be the centerpiece of a democracy? Why?

Can you see the sacred value in suffering? What purpose does it have for you and what does it give you?

Our past lets go of us when we are able to find deeper meanings in the experiences. What steps can you take to make meaning of the sufferings you've experienced? Can the experience of suffering deepen your life? If so, how?

ISRAEL

EZEKIEL AND HIS VISION OF THE HOLY CITY WITHIN

We are expanding our understanding of the Axial Age, this period of enormous spiritual development which covered approximately 800 years, from 900 BCE to 200 BCE, and left an indelible mark on the principle spiritual foundations of nearly all the religious traditions that are present in the world today. Judaism, Christianity, and Islam, the three major religions of the world, are the flowering of the Axial Age experienced by the confederation of tribes called Israel. The Israelites appeared in the highlands of Canaan after the mysterious disintegration of both the Egyptian and Hittite kingdoms that had ruled the Near East for centuries. "Shortly before 1200 (BCE), a network of new settlements were established in the highlands, stretching from the lower Galilee in the north to Beersheba in the south" (Armstrong, 2006, p. 44). The first mention of these non-imposing villages, which had modest houses and whose economy was based on cereal crops and herding, was in a victory stele of Pharaoh Mernepteh (c. 1210 BCE) (Armstrong, 2006, p. 44). These were the tribes, the people of Israel.

The story of Israel's origins would become the organizing symbol from which its Axial vision of monotheism would break through (Armstrong, 2006, p. 45). The Bible is a product of their Axial Age, and it took several centuries for it to be written and finalized in the version we know today. The definitive narrative of their saga had been changed, embroidered, reinterpreted, and expanded many times over. The patriarchs of the religion were Abraham, Moses, Joshua, and David. One of the most important and influential of these founding stories is the liberation from Egypt. The god of Israel, Yahweh, taking pity on his people after being enslaved by the Egyptians for 400 years, freed them, and under the leadership of Moses, parted the Red Sea, drowned the Egyptian army, made a covenant on Mount Sinai, and provided them with the Ten Commandments. In order to purge themselves, the Israelites were forced by their god to wander through the desert for 40 years before they could enter the Promised Land. Moses died prior to their arrival. Joshua took over, crossed the river Jordan, and defeated the Canaanite armies arrayed against them. So the story goes.

However, the excavations of Israel since the late 1960's show no archeological sign of this having taken place. "They have found no trace of the mass destruction described in the book of Joshua, no signs of foreign invasion, no Egyptian artifacts, and no indication of a change in population" (Armstrong, 2006, p. 46). What we know, based on the evidence, is that the early biblical writers weren't trying to write a historically accurate account; "They were searching for the meaning of existence. These were epic stories, national sagas that helped the people to create a distinct identity" (Armstrong, 2006, p. 46).

Life was extremely violent in the highlands. Israel was born out of trauma and upheaval, and they needed to develop an identity to unite the tribes. Thus, they began their unique relationship with their god, Yahweh. Yahweh was a warrior god, and gave strength and courage to a people beleaguered by war from all fronts. He was but one of many gods that people worshipped in the area. Yahweh was among the sons of El, the high god of Canaan, and even Abraham, Isaac, and Jacob had worshipped El (Armstrong, 2006, p. 48). Other gods that Yahweh had to compete with were the storm god Baal; Marduk was another. These too, were warrior gods, their stories were mythic and filled with wars that convulsed the cosmos and shattered the earth. The violent, dangerous lives of the peoples in these territories needed the support of their divine warrior gods. "War was a sanctified activity" (Armstrong, 2006, p. 52). Preparing for battle was a religious experience, and the warriors would purify themselves with the same devotion as they would for any of their sacred rites. The battlefield was holy ground, where the god would be leading and fighting alongside his people. Such were the early times of the tribes of Israel.

The Israelites had worshipped many other gods besides Yahweh. It wasn't until the prophet Elijah (whose name means "Yahweh is my God!") that someone insisted, on record, the exclusive worship of Yahweh (Armstrong, 2006, p. 75). This was a major breakthrough of their Axial Age, however, it did not come easily. The cult of Yahweh was gradually becoming more peaceful; but the fiery words of repentance and submission to Yahweh still remained. To cast off all other gods, some very beloved by the people, and give your heart to the one God of Israel, required courage and faith that Yahweh would provide in all situations and circumstances.

"Axial Age religion would be conditioned by a sympathy that enabled people to *feel with* others" (Armstrong, 2006, p. 105). This concept of empathy for others, along with another axial ideal of spiritual self-surrender, was often preceded by suffering. Indeed, the history of the early Israelites is loaded with suffering, violence, and trauma. The evolution to monotheism would take the people, the prophets, and the kings of Israel through many dark times. The sixth century BCE would test the faith of the Israelites in their God. The catalyst for change was again unrestrained violence and war. The Babylonian King Nebuchadnezzar had invaded the kingdom of Judah (a little historical note: the Israelites after King Solomon had divided themselves into two kingdoms, Israel in the north, and Judah in the south. The kingdom of Israel had been vanquished earlier in 722 BCE by the Assyrian king, Shalmaneser V) (Armstrong, 2006, p. 117). With his superior army, King Nebuchadnezzar defeated the Israelites, subjugated the region, and exiled thousands to Babylon. The suffering experienced by the Israelites during this period of exile was very intense. Many of those left behind after the destructive fury of the Babylonian army lived in misery. Jerusalem was in ruins. "People clawed at garbage dumps for food, mothers killed and boiled their babies, and handsome young men roamed the ruined streets with blackened faces and skeletal bodies" (Armstrong, 2006, p. 198). The people of Israel had lost everything. Humiliated and filled with despair, they stood collectively on the edge of a cliff and stared into the great terrifying abyss. Yahweh had been worsted, defeated by the god of Babylon, Marduk. The people lost all hope. Many were seeking answers and turning within to find an explanation why their God had abandoned them. This turn to the interior, seeing things exactly as they were, and taking individual responsibility for their erroneous ways would create a new, deeper, and more personal understanding of, and relationship with the God of Israel. One of the principle players in this radical transformation was the prophet Ezekiel.

THE PROPHET EZEKIEL

Ezekiel was a young priest when he was deported to Babylon in 597 BCE (he eventually settled in Tel Aviv). He had a succession of powerful visions that would lead him through the profound agony of his suffering into a more peaceful, inner spirituality. Just five years into his exile, Ezekiel had a vision where he saw a being that looked like Yahweh sitting on a throne in a war chariot holding onto a scroll. Written on this scroll were all the lamentations of the people, and "Ezekiel was forced to eat it, painfully assimilating the violence and sorrow of his time" (Armstrong, 2006, p. 203). Why would God want Ezekiel to eat the sorrows of his people? This made no sense. His vision was beyond rational comprehension or explanation. Yet, when Ezekiel ate the scroll, allowed himself to experience the full weight of the grief, sorrow, fear, and pain, "he found that "it tasted as sweet as honey"" (Armstrong, 2006, p. 204).

Ezekiel believed the Judeans' world had been turned on its head as a consequence of idolatry, immorality, and wickedness on the part of the Judeans, and not on some external enemy. The enemy was only doing God's will. Yahweh – God – had left them; he would bring no comfort, but would remain with them in exile until they repented. They must rid themselves of all delusions, reform from within, and be brutally honest about their own failings. "Instead of blaming the Babylonians for their cruelty, projecting their pain onto the enemy, Ezekiel forced his fellow exiles to look nearer home" (Armstrong, 2006, p. 206). He was asking them to examine their own sinfulness and where they had gone astray. Let me remind the reader that sin is an archery term and means you've 'missed the mark'. When we miss the mark, we need to correct our aim. Repenting our sins is recognizing when we haven't been following the guidance from our hearts, have violated the law in our souls, and feel deep sorrow for the actions we've taken. Suffering occurred in this context as a consequence of the iniquitous actions and behaviors of the Judeans. Ezekiel implored his fellow exiles to take responsibility for their own actions, and with a full heart, experience the totality of their sorrow. Only this would help them to realign with the ways of their God.

After exile and full repentance, Yahweh would bring them back home. In another vision, the 'Valley of the Bones' vision, Ezekiel watched as Yahweh breathed life back into the bones lying in the desert. These bones represented the exiled community. "A new heart also will I give you, and a new spirit will I put within you, and I will take away the stony heart out of your flesh, and I will give you a heart of flesh" (Ezekiel 36:26). The restoration of the exiles in Jerusalem would happen because Ezekiel and others "had assimilated their pain, acknowledged their own responsibility, and allowed their hearts to break, they had become humane" (Armstrong, 2006, p. 206).

Following the destruction of Jerusalem, Ezekiel, near the end of his life, had a final temple vision of a city called Yahweh Sham, which means "Yahweh is there!" (Armstrong, 2006, p. 206). The city was situated on a high mountain. It was a new commonwealth that surrounded a new temple, with Yahweh at the center. God had returned, if only in the prophet's mind. Ezekiel saw an earthly paradise: a temple situated in the heart of the city; rivers bubbled up and flowed out of the sanctuary, down the sacred mountain, bringing life and healing to all who lived there. "The temple was the nucleus of the whole world; divine power radiated from it to the land and people of Israel in a series of concentric circles" (Armstrong, 2006, p. 207). Despite the fact that Jerusalem lay in ruins, the holy city within still lived and was never out of one's reach. Ezekiel had made the temple an internal reality, similar to what they were doing in India with the mandala. It was a symbol of meditation, "an image of the properly ordered life, centered on the divine" (Armstrong, 2006, p. 207). It is likely that when Ezekiel and his disciples meditated on the holy city within, a replication of the temple that had once stood, they were orienting themselves to their larger Self, and, "some were discovering a divine presence at the core of their being" (Armstrong, 2006, p. 208).

'THE HOLY CITY WITHIN' MEDITATION

In this moment, feel the breath of God breathe new life into your bones. "I will put my breath into you and you shall live again, and I will set you upon your own soil" (Ezekiel 37:14). The soil is the ground of your life centered on the divine. Your true center. The true center of us all, our core, the essence of our being. Feel yourself renewed, refreshed, and re-vitalized by the breath of new life. Your bodies are restored, your bodies are strengthened and healed, your heart filled with love, compassion, and empathy for all life and for yourself.

Walk along the path to the Holy City within. The path is shown you. It is not difficult to walk. Notice how light and free you are. The birds are singing, the branches of the trees wave to you as you pass by, the animals greet you along the way. All is love. All is joy. All is pure. All is peaceful. As you come around the bend, you catch a glimpse of the magnificent city within, within you, situated high on the mountain. The white marble buildings sparkle with delight as they greet you with a shower of dancing lights reflecting the rays of the golden sun above. It takes your breath away. Its holiness radiates such warmth, peace, love, and joy. It's unlike anything you have ever experienced. Your eyes fill with tears, tears of joy, to stand in the presence of pure beauty. This is you. This is your Holy City within.

An angel appears to escort you high into the air, and carry you to the heart of this magnificent city. To its temple. The holiest of holies. This temple within. You soar above the city. It is teeming with life, abundance, joy, and laughter. The people below see you in the air and wave joyfully at you, welcoming you to your right-ful home. The sky is resplendent. So clear. So blue. No clouds in the sky. The air whisks past your face, refreshing you and filling up your heart with joy. "I'm home. I've finally come home," you say to yourself.

The angel points to where the temple is. Large marble col-umns, beautiful gardens all around; you are looking at an earthly paradise. The angel gently brings you down into this paradise. This paradise within. Around the temple, you see a beautiful river that flows around and through the garden. You see how this river flows out beyond the gardens, out into the city, down the sacred mountain, bringing life, healing, and abundance to the people and the countryside. The Holiness which emanates from this temple blesses the entire world, and you are its center.

You move toward the temple. Inside the temple, an eternal fire burns in the very center. This tower of fire living in the temple of your heart never dies, never goes away, always radiating its pure white light within you, the source of your own divine presence. This presence is at the very core of your being. Stand in awe, gratitude, and love in the presence of who and what you are at the very core of your being. You are among the sons and daughters of God. This is your temple. This is your version of the Holy City within. The kingdom of God is within, it is here, and now you come to know the truth.

While standing here in the temple of your Holy City within, let us take 5 breaths in silence, and breathe in the Holiness at the core of your being.

And on your last breath, see the temple, see the burning fire within, see the gardens, the river, the flowers, the trees, the birds, and all of the marvels of your beautiful city and sanctuary. This is your true home. May it be a place of comfort, joy, love, and peace to you whenever you may need it.

Gently now, come back into the room, and when you are ready, open your eyes.

WORKBOOK QUESTIONS ON EZEKIEL AND THE HOLY CITY WITHIN

What can we learn about our own suffering through the story of Ezekiel?

How can you assimilate your pain, take responsibility for your part that you played in your story, and forgive those who need to be forgiven, including yourself? Is it possible? Why or why not?

What are your impressions of Yahweh? Do you think our conception of God evolves as we evolve?

Why do you think so many prophets, mystics, and sages of the past speak about the silence that follows after life's many storms? What mystery could you find if you cultivated a relationship with the silence? Does this have value for you?

Draw a picture of your Holy City within or maybe your Garden of Eden. Have fun with it!

CHINA

LAO TZU: THE THREE GREATEST TREASURES

China's Axial Age developed independently from the other regions experiencing a spiritual revolution. Isolated by high mountains and swampy, uninhabitable land, the great plain of China made it difficult for civilization to take root. "The climate was harsh, with broiling summers and icy winters, when settlements were attacked by freezing, sand-laden winds. The Yellow River was difficult to navigate and prone to flooding" (Armstrong, 2006, p. 31). The earliest settlers of the great plain date back to at least the third millennium BCE. The feudal kings who ruled this period tamed the countryside and made it inhabitable. They drained the swamps, built dikes, led the rivers to the sea, and developed agriculture. The sage kings who wrestled power from nature and the universal order, established their kingdoms, and made the countryside habitable, would serve as "an inspiration to the philosophers of the Chinese Axial Age" (Armstrong, 2006, p. 31).

The history of China is replete with the rise and fall of numerous dynasties. If Heaven favored a particular ruler, his dynasty would rise as a consequence of the Mandate of Heaven. This concept was first introduced by the duke of Zhou (11th Century BCE). He was searching for a solution as to why the people of China should follow the new king after the Zhou had seized power from the Shang dynasty. To be king, one had to receive the blessings of Di, the High God, and be invested with the power from Heaven to govern and to rule. The previous dynasty had lost the mandate because they had oppressed their subjects. They had lost the Way, and the people were suffering as a consequence. Justice needed to be reestablished and the Zhou, because of their virtuous ruler, had been consecrated as the rightful king. A king would lose his right to rule if he was cruel and merciless. But, if the ruler "was wise, humane, and truly concerned for the welfare of his subjects, people would flock to him from all over the world, and Heaven would raise him to the highest position" (Armstrong, 2006, p. 41). The idea of the Mandate of Heaven would become a central ideal to the philosophers of the Chinese Axial Age.

In order to preserve the Way (dao) of Heaven, the Chinese created elaborate rituals to ensure and sustain the natural order of things here on earth. Heaven and earth were not separated as they were in other religious traditions like the cult of Yahweh or the Greek pantheon of Gods and Goddesses. Rather, Heaven and earth coexisted together simultaneously, complementing each other in a balanced, harmonious relationship. Humans continued and contributed to the completion of the creation Heaven had begun. This continuum allowed for humans to share in the divine process; all acts were considered sacred, and either supported the Way or maligned it. The king was invested with the royal mandate. If he followed the Way correctly, his kingdom flourished. If he did not, there would be chaos, disorder, followed by decline.

Ritual (li) played an instrumental part in the spiritual life of the Chinese. If one followed the li perfectly, understood the value and significance of what they were doing, why they were doing it, and performed the ritual correctly, the Way of Heaven would be preserved. Initially, only the kings performed these rituals. But as the monarchy of the Zhou dynasty inevitably declined, others were permitted to participate as the political, social, and economic landscape changed. The *junzi* ("the gentleman") of the aristocratic warrior class increasingly became preoccupied with the *li* (Armstrong, 2006, p. 136). By infusing their minds with the sacred traditions encoded in the *li*, it was believed to promote self-control, moderation, reverence, and respect. If all the families and clans of China followed the *li*, harmony and peace would reign. This idea was based on a sagacious psychological insight. "When people are consistently treated with the utmost respect, they learn to feel worthy of reverence; they realize they have absolute value" (Armstrong, 2006, p. 174).

However, toward the end of the sixth century BCE, China was thrown into crisis. The region became engulfed in warfare as the separate principalities challenged one another for territory, the destruction of the enemy, and dominance. The constraints imposed by tradition were disintegrating because the rule of the descendants of the duke of Zhou and the old baronial families was in decline, "and China seemed to be rushing headlong into anarchy" (Armstrong, 2006, p. 237). Greed, power, aggression, violence, and materialism threatened to destroy the sacredness and sanctity of life that had been established by the Way of Heaven. The cosmic balance and interdependence between Heaven and earth was in jeopardy. The lives of all the Chinese people were endangered if they could not be brought back to the Way. It was under these severe conditions that China's Axial Age began.

Confucius was among the first philosophers to begin teaching others how to return to the sacred path of the Way. He felt the Way was accessible to all, to everyone. A *junzi*, the true gentleman, was not a warrior, but a scholar (Armstrong, 2006, p. 241), and everyone had the potential within him to become one. By studying and treading the sacred path carefully, enthusiastically, one would learn how to be good here, transcend the limitations imposed on him by his society and circumstances, and evolve into a profoundly mature and spiritual being. In order to submit to altruism and surrender the ego's pettiness, cruelty, and selfishness, people needed to become fully aware, fully conscious of their actions. Self-transcendence occurred when people felt empathy with others. This lesson was learned and cultivated by treating others with respect. By nourishing the holiness in others, they would naturally bring out the holiness in you. "Never do to others what you would not like them to do to you" (Armstrong, 2006, p. 247). This was the Way: the Golden Rule. Confucius was the first to spread the message of this singular virtue. He believed that if people constantly behaved in this way, wars would end or never start; exploitation of the masses would end; hatred, cruelty, and opposition would dissolve away. It required a life-long struggle to master, "but if you did so, you achieved a moral power that was almost tangible" (Armstrong, 2006, p. 250).

Despite Confucius' noble efforts to infuse Chinese society with the compassionate and pragmatic spirit of the Golden Rule, shortly after his death, China descended again into a violent and frightening era in their long history. This period historians have defined as 'the Period of the Warring States', which started around 485 BCE and ended in the year 221 BCE (Armstrong, 2006, p. 316). "The Warring States era was one of those rare periods of history when a succession of changes, each reinforcing the other, accelerates the process of development, and leads to a fundamental alteration of society" (Armstrong, 2006, p. 317). During this period, warfare was transformed from a ritualized display of courtly warriors, each competing with each other for moderation, generosity, and courtesy, to one where campaigns were aimed at the destruction and subjugation of the other states. The victorious army would confiscate their lands and resources, and wipe out the enemy, including women, the elderly, and children. As military technology advanced, killing techniques and weaponry became more lethal. Large armies were assembled from the peasant population, who, at one time, had only been on the periphery of feudal warfare. Violence, brutality, and aggression erupted on the great plain of China like never before, altering the social, political, economic, and intellectual life of every Chinese. These disturbing trends galvanized the deep thinkers and sages to renew their quest for a peaceful solution to China's rampant militancy and aggression.

One of the many Chinese philosophers, who, at this time, were trying to encourage sympathy with the enemy and a returning of individuals back into harmony with the Way in the hopes of bringing an end to the terrifying wars tearing apart the country, was Zhuangzi. Zhuangzi was a hermit who had abandoned public life. While searching for peace, he discovered one day while hunting, it was impossible for creatures to be entirely and absolutely safe. He was hunting a magpie, who didn't notice him, and this magpie was hunting a cicada, which was also being hunted by a preying mantis. All creatures seemed to be programmed to hunt one another, whether they were aware of it or not. This recognition haunted and depressed Zhuangzi. "We were conditioned to destroy and be destroyed, to eat and be eaten. We could not escape our destiny. Until we became reconciled to the endless process of destruction and dissolution, we would have no peace" (Armstrong, 2006, p. 351).

This incident in the park opened Zhuangzi's mind to a wider understanding of the world, how it is structured and how it operates. He learned life is constantly and forever in a state of change; things rise and they fall; everything is moving toward becoming something else and it was a futile effort to resist these changes built into the universe. The cycles of creation, destruction, and creation again was how the Way of Heaven worked. If one could reconcile themselves to this unalterable truth of the world, this endless cycle of transformation going on in the cosmos, it was possible to attain freedom from the fear of death. This, in itself, would be a liberating experience. Zhuangzi's enlightenment was rooted in a balanced, perfect acceptance of the axis around which life revolved. Surrendering his egoistic desires to preserve his life at all costs and flow with the Way, Zhuangzi could live "with cheerful interest and detachment, and remain calm and content" (Armstrong, 2006, p. 353). Peace could be attained by attuning oneself to the reality of the Way of Heaven.

LAO TZU

The last of the great sages of China's Axial Age was Lao Tzu. Legend describes how Lao Tzu, (which translates to "Old Master"), when he was very old, left China on a water buffalo and headed to the West. He was exceedingly disappointed and saddened at the political situation going on in the Chou province, and the violence, greed, and vanity of men. Mankind had fallen away from his natural goodness by the constant busy-ness of his *yu wei* (shaping desire into action) mind. He was stopped along the road by a guard who recognized him and asked Lao Tzu to compose his teachings. The epitome of selfless compassion for the plight of humanity, Lao Tzu relented, and composed what is known to us as the *Daodejing* (http://www.notablebiographies.com/Ki-Lo/Lao-Tzu.html, http://www.iep.utm.edu/laozi/#H4). This ancient text of how an individual may access the Way of Heaven through interior reflection on one's own spirituality translates as the "*Classic of the Way and Its Potency*" (Armstrong, 2006, p. 406).

The *Daodejing* begins with these lines:

The Tao that can be spoken is not the eternal Tao

The name that can be named is not the eternal name

The nameless is the origin of Heaven and Earth

(http://www.taoism.net/ttc/complete.htm)

It consists of eighty-one chapters written in verse that are elusive and paradoxical. These contradictions were intended, as the student must learn to hold them together in his heart to understand the true nature of reality. Our constant pursuit of desires kept us from knowing the *dao*, which was the unseen, all-powerful, fundamental source of existence. The source of our existence could only be found by acting counterintuitively with the rest of the world. An individual must desist in planning, organizing, and structuring his life based on the beliefs and laws of the society. He must empty his mind of all thoughts, calm and relax his body, and practice the discipline of *wu wei* (do nothing). In this way, by rooting oneself deeply with the source of all life, one was connected to the fertile Void, and with this accomplished within the individual, everything was effortlessly accomplished in the physical realm.

> The sage ruler must behave like Heaven, which pursued its own inscrutable course without interfering with the Ways of other creatures. This is the Way things ought to be, and this – not ceaseless, purposeful activism – would bring peace to the world. (Armstrong, 2006, pp. 410 – 411)
>
> In Chapter 67 of the *Daodejing*, Lao Tzu writes:
>
> *I have three treasures*
>
> *I hold onto them and protect them*
>
> *The first is called compassion*
>
> *The second is called conservation* (simplicity)
>
> *The third is called not daring to be ahead in the world* (patience)
>
> (http://www.taoism.net/ttc/complete.htm)

Depending upon the translation read, essentially, the three greatest treasures Lao Tzu could teach us is simplicity, patience, and compassion. Simplicity is the idea that when we are simple in our thoughts and actions, we come closer to the source of our being. Our simplest pleasures are usually the ones which bring us the most joy. When our *yu wei* mind drives us incessantly to achieve and crave more, we lose touch with our essential nature and become defined by worldly expectations. This feeds our ego's need to compare and compete with others. Consequently, we treat others with contempt, and we treat ourselves harshly for not meeting up with the demands of our inexhaustible pursuits. Simplicity returns us to the basics, where our thoughts and actions go hand-in-hand with our individual nature, before civilization interfered with it. The simpler we get, the more honest, authentic, and true we are to ourselves and to others.

Patience is the second great treasure, and this virtue can be very challenging to cultivate. When someone provokes us, it's very easy to react with another attack. This habituated response becomes an invitation to another act of aggression, and thus, the cycle of violence continues. Patience asks you to refrain and to absorb hostility; to wait until your mind settles down and the emotions have cleared. When we are patient with both our friends and our enemies, practicing *wu wei* or "do nothing", we remain in harmony with the way things are. Patience can be cultivated by recognizing that people have faults. This is a universal phenomenon of all people, including you and me. When we recognize our own faults in others – how impatient, rude, quick to anger, or vain we can be – we begin to nurture patience in dealing with someone exhibiting these same faults. Patience helps us to be at ease with reality, accepting reality as it is, and being one with it. It also gives us a chance to preserve our integrity when challenged by a person or situation until the right action arises all by itself.

The third treasure is compassion. This virtue's essence means that we suffer together. By identifying sympathetically with the suffering and misfortune of another, combined with a strong desire to help alleviate the emotional, physical, or spiritual pains of the person or group, we develop empathy, or a concern for others.

Frequently though, we forget to be compassionate toward ourselves. We may be excessively hard, making unkind demands or expecting too much. This often is reflected back to us in how we treat others. Having self-compassion – learning to express loving thoughts about who we are; being kind and gentle; and treating ourselves the way we want and deserve to be treated – teaches us compassion. We are then able to extend compassion to others, treating them with love, kindness, respect, and honor. We learn to reconcile all beings in this Way because we begin to understand we are not so different from each other. Compassion draws us closer to our hearts through our small acts of loving-kindness. This is the key to healing our broken world. As Karen Armstrong points out in the last sentence of her book, "we need...to go in search of the lost heart, the spirit of compassion that lies at the core of all our traditions" (Armstrong, 2006, p. 476).

MEDITATION ON SIMPLICITY

In your mind's eye, go to your favorite spot – one that fills you with peace, serenity, and joy. Perhaps it's a park near your home, your backyard, near a lake in the mountains, a quiet spot on the beach. Place yourself fully there. Empty your mind. When thoughts come in, thank them, and let them go. Just be. Be in this place, this sanctuary; this slice of heaven.

Notice your surroundings. Take it all in. Notice the different colors, the shades of green on the trees, the shapes of the trees, the bark, the size of the trunk, the little branches that protrude out as your eyes wander up to the sky. See the branches that extend from the trunk – follow these branches all the way out to the stems, then to the leaves, and then stop on one particular leaf. Notice it. Notice the simplicity of life in this tree. It's perfect. Nothing out of place. Breathe in this simplicity.

Your eyes catch sight of a butterfly. Watch as the butterfly dances from branch to branch, floating on the air in a zig-zag pattern, its dance of life, of joy, of love. Not one of its actions is wasted. It flutters high, then low, then high again – this dance in the breathless wind until it lands beside you on a beautiful flower. The flower could be a rose, a sunflower, an orchid, whatever flower comes up for you, that's the flower for you. See the butterfly open and close its wings. Just be with this image, this experience. Empty your mind of everything else. Feel and notice the simplicity of life connected to this butterfly and flower. It's through our conscious acts to be self-aware in the moments of life that we see and experience its beauty, simplicity, and vitality.

The butterfly flutters, bounces away, dancing its dance of freedom on the breathless wind; your heart fills with joy. There is nothing to do, nowhere to go. If you pay attention, all of life unfolds before you. Feel the peace welling up inside, this inner calm…the sense of being inexplicably connected to all that is around you. You notice another butterfly, and another, until you become aware the whole tree is filled with these beautiful, delicate creatures. The whole tree is alive with the dancing butterflies. The ancient Greeks thought that the butterfly was a symbol for the soul. A liberated soul, free from the constraints and pressures of our lives, is like these butterflies – dancing in the wind, connected to the mystery and sacredness of life. Breathe this in. Hear the sounds of the birds chirping around you. Feel the wind brushing up caressingly against your legs. Empty your mind and just be. You hear the sound of a child laughing in the distance. Notice how easy and simple it is to feel fully alive in the present moment.

There's nothing to do. There's nowhere to go. Simply BE. All of it gets done. Breathe this in for 5 long breaths in silence.

And on your last breath, before we open our eyes, I want to leave you with a quote from Lao Tzu: "Be content with what you have; rejoice in the way things are. When you realize there is nothing lacking, the whole world belongs to you" (http://www.brainy-quote.com/quotes/quotes/l/laotzu393061.html).

Gently, when you are ready, come back into the room, and open your eyes.

WORKBOOK QUESTIONS ON LAO TZU AND SIMPLICITY

How can you practice in your daily life the virtue of simplicity?

In your own words, what do you think the *dao* is?

Why would Lao Tzu want you to "do nothing" in order to receive everything? What is he trying to get you to understand?

Are you content with what you have? In what ways could you learn to rejoice in the way things are? What's the value in seeing life in this Way?

PATIENCE MEDITATION

In your mind's eye, I want you to go to a place that deeply connects you to nature. Maybe this is next to a lake or a pond; maybe this is by a babbling brook hidden in a beautiful valley surrounded by majestic, white-capped mountains; or maybe this is a quiet spot on the beach where the waves roll in one after the other in an endless rhythm that brings you serenity and calm. Place your whole self – there. Feel the environment with all your senses. Go there and just BE.

See how nature in all its glory accomplishes everything without coercing it, not forcing itself to be something, or rushing into something because it has to do it. Everything flows; everything is in harmony, everything is in balance. Consider and contemplate in this space the cycle of life. A tree begins as an acorn, a seed which you can hold in your hand. When you plant it, something miraculous happens, it breaks open, roots shoot out of it, and out of the ground emerges a new sapling. All of its potential was in the acorn. Patiently, it moves from one stage of life to the next. It's not in any rush. It doesn't have to be in a hurry. It follows what's inherent in its own nature. To grow. To become a tree. Watch it grow. See how it passes through the seasons. How it faces and weathers the winters, blooms in the spring, delights in life during the summers, and sheds its skin in the fall. Watch as this happens season after season; year after year. The trunk gets wider and wider; the tree gets taller and taller; the branches stretch out farther and farther. Notice how nature's will is accomplished without having to do anything but be what it is. Patiently it grew. Patiently it endured. Patiently it became what it was always meant to be.

Now apply this metaphor into your own life. Notice times in your life when you acted impatiently – how it increased your stress, how you felt this internal pressure to get something done, how it may have agitated you or caused you to react angrily toward someone, and remember what that feeling was like. See yourself in this situation. Now imagine yourself cultivating the attitude of patience. See how you are able to absorb whatever feelings and emotions are going on around you, not taking anything personally, just trusting in your own inner nature. Being patient until the right solution comes to mind. When we are patient, the right solution comes. When we are patient, we don't overreact to situations or people in our lives. We are steady, following that same rhythm we see in nature; the same rhythm, the same divine intelligence, which can transform an acorn into an oak tree and an embryo into a baby. Patience allows us to enjoy the moments of life as they happen instead of rushing by them. When we learn to cultivate patience, we return to our roots, back to our true essence and natural rhythm of life; back to our true selves. We will simply Be.

See this place again. See how nature patiently and in its own time accomplishes everything. Nothing is ever wasted. Everything lives according to its essence – whether that's a tree, a flower, an insect, or a bird. Know that you are a part of this. Feel the essence that animates all of life living inside of you. Empty your mind. Feel the essence of life burning bright inside of you. It is through patience that we are brought back to who we are because when we "do nothing" and give ourselves the time to allow things to happen on and of their own accord, all gets accomplished in harmony with the Way, the Way of Heaven.

In this space of being aligned with your true Way, let us breathe in silence for 5 breaths.

Lao Tzu said, "Do you have the patience to wait until your mind settles and the water is clear? Can you remain unmoving until the right action arises by itself?" (http://www.goodreads.com/quotes/341604-do-you-have-the-patience-to-wait-till-your-mud)

With patience in our minds, let us come back into the room, and when you are ready, gently, open your eyes.

WORKBOOK QUESTIONS ON PATIENCE

What does patience mean to you? Do you see the value it has in your life? Give examples.

Have you ever acted with impatience in a situation and then regretted it? Describe what happened and how the result might have been different if you would have patiently waited for the right action to arise.

What lessons can we learn from nature about patience? Find an example from nature and use it as a metaphor for an example in your own life.

Describe, in your own words, the Way of Heaven.

COMPASSION MEDITATION

Place your hand, your right hand on your heart. Feel its beating underneath your hand together with the gentle rise and fall of your breathing. Feel and notice this inescapable harmony lying beneath the surface of all your thoughts, feelings, emotions, beliefs, pains, sufferings, and traumas. This beautiful harmony that regulates and balances your life, no matter what the circumstances may be, to keep the gift of life with you always. The heart beats and beats without you having to do or say anything. The heart has intelligence beyond words and comprehension. It's where the truth of you lives, the divine spark, the light of the world, and it is our hearts that allow us to move into the space of empathy and compassion...the desire to alleviate the suffering of others.

Now, I want you to imagine someone you love. Someone who the mere thought of fills your heart with so much love and compassion. See them standing before you smiling. Your heart swells with gratitude for their being in your life. Notice intuitively how you wish to alleviate their suffering, how easy it is to feel compassion for this person. Allow this feeling to fill up every cell of your being. And now, I want you to repeat this in your mind as you extend compassion to your beloved person: "May you be well. May you be free of pain and suffering. May the light of the world protect you always." (Repeat twice). See them smile. Feel the love they have for you pouring out of their heart like a beam of light into yours. See the light of the world fill them up with this divine essence. Notice how connected you truly are.

Now, standing next to this person whom you love and is so easy to extend compassion toward, is someone who evokes the opposite feeling. Perhaps this is a person who has hurt you deeply and you feel you can never forgive them; perhaps this person has caused immeasurable suffering on humanity – if it's too difficult with this person, choose someone else who has caused you pain that you can extend compassion toward. As Christ said, it is easy to love our friends, we must do the same toward those we consider enemies. See this person. Acknowledge all the pain and suffering they may have caused you, and again, let us extend an offering of compassion for their struggles: "May you be well. May you be free of pain and suffering. May the light of the world heal you." (Repeat twice). Thank both of these persons for coming into your consciousness and giving you the opportunity to extend compassion.

And just as our friend and our enemy need our compassion, let us take a moment and turn our attention to ourselves, who need it just as much. "May I be well. May I be free of pain and suffering. May the light of the world heal all my wounds and protect me always." (Repeat twice).

And now, let us move beyond ourselves, beyond our homes, our cities, our nations. Seeing the whole world in our mind's eye, let us extend our compassion to the world, a world we all hope to one day live in perfect peace: "May we all be well. May we all be free of pain and suffering. May the light of the world heal all our wounds and bring peace to all peoples of the world." (Repeat twice).

In this space of unlimited compassion, let us take a moment to breathe in this space in silence for 5 deep breaths.

Lao Tzu said,

If there is to be peace in the world,

There must be peace in the nations.

If there is to be peace in the nations,

There must be peace in the cities.

If there is to be peace in the cities,

There must be peace between neighbors.

If there is to be peace between neighbors,

There must be peace in the home.

If there is to be peace in the home,

There must be peace in the heart.

(http://www.goodreads.com/
quotes/125184-if-there-is-to-be-peace-in-the-world-there)

Let us carry this message into our daily life. Slowly, come back into the room, and when you are ready, gently, open your eyes.

WORKBOOK QUESTIONS ON COMPASSION

What does compassion mean to you? Give examples of how you have been compassionate.

It's hard to feel compassion for someone who has hurt us. It's much easier to hold a grievance against them. How does holding a grievance against them serve you? Does it add to your life? Can you think of reasons why it would be good to let go of the grievance? (This doesn't mean what they did was right, this is about freeing your heart from the pains of the past.)

How have you been kind and gentle with yourself? In what ways have you expressed self-compassion?

What does peace mean to you? What does it look like?

INDIA

THE UPANISHADS

We are now turning our attention to the Axial Age of India, which gave rise to modern day Hinduism and Buddhism, and whose mystics and luminaries pushed forward the frontiers of awareness and human consciousness. We, as a world community, are indebted to these mystics, sages, philosophers, and poets who were seeking to discover the transcendental dimension of existence in the core of a human being. Prior to this great inner transformation, God, or the divine in its many manifestations, was experienced through rituals, sacred dramas, and animal sacrifice. The Axial Age masters changed this. They still valued ritual, but placed ethics and morality as the preeminent factor for experiencing the divine in our life. Compassion was religion. A person committed to the spiritual life was concerned for and respected the sacred human rights of all beings. Those who originally shaped our religious traditions wanted to create a peaceful world by first transforming the individual.

All the sages preached a spirituality of empathy and compassion; they insisted that people must abandon their egotism and greed, their violence and unkindness. Not only was it wrong to kill another human being; you must not even speak a hostile word or make an irritable gesture. Further, nearly all the Axial sages realized that you could not confine your benevolence to your own people: your concern must somehow extend to the entire world. (Armstrong, 2006, pp. xviii – xix)

Through the kindness and generosity manifested by our thoughts, words, and deeds – each person doing their individual part, the world would be saved.

India was in the vanguard of the Axial Age spiritual revolution. Between 1500 BCE – 1000 BCE, the Indus Valley had been infiltrated through a series of migrations by the Sanskrit-speaking Aryans, a tribe of people that originated on the Caucasian steppes of southern Russia. Their name "meant something like "noble" or "honorable"" (Armstrong, 2006, p. 1). Before coming to India, they had been shepherds tending livestock, and lived a quiet, pastoral life. However, as a consequence of the discovery of new technology and new weaponry from neighboring advanced societies, some of these early Aryans surrendered their peaceful ways, and became warriors. Violence erupted on the Steppes, cattle rustlers were killing, plundering, and raping the frightened villagers, and their humble way of life was turned upside down. The world of the Aryans had suddenly become polarized, with good fighting against evil. A wave of aggressive, unprecedented violence destroyed the peaceful existence of life on the Steppes, and the Aryan cattle rustlers who migrated southeast would carry this warrior ethos with them into India.

The Aryan immigrants wanted a dynamic religion. They were cattle rustlers; the god they worshipped was Indra, who with his wild flowing beard and his passion for battle, was the archetypal warrior god that gave their warring a sacred dimension. By making war a sacred experience, the Aryans were able to feel the rage, heat, and glory of the god. It was a demonic frenzy, a burning heat that the warriors were seeking. "...the wrath of the young warrior, which manifests itself in extreme heat, is a magico-religious experience; there is nothing profane or natural about it – it is the syndrome of gaining possession of a sacrality" (Eliade, 1958, p. 85). In order to survive, to conquer, to dominate, and to ultimately subdue the region, the Aryans turned war into a ritual. "When they fought, they became more than themselves and felt united with Indra; these rituals gave their warfare a "soul," and by linking their earthly battles with the divine archetype, they made them holy" (Armstrong, 2006, p. 20). This warrior ethos permeated every layer of their society. Violence, aggression, bloody sacrifices, fiercely competitive ritual contests, glory, and terror were the dominating features of this period of history in this part of India.

As Aryan life became more settled and the economy more agricultural, there was an emerging consensus that the destructive cycle of violence that characterized their society had to end. The priestly class began reforming their rites and rituals, taking out the violence, and moving toward a concept that would become an indispensable virtue of India's Axial Age. The ideal these reformists were inspired by was the concept of *ahimsa*, which means harmlessness (Armstrong, 2006, p. 92). The re-direction of the spiritual life by these mystics was aimed at the discovery of the interior world, and the connection to the 'atman'. The 'atman' would "refer to the essential and eternal core of the human person, which made him or her unique" (Armstrong, 2006, p. 98). In the Svetasvatara Upanishad, the Atman is described as such:

Concealed in the heart of all beings lies the Atman, the Spirit, the Self; smaller than the smallest atom, greater than the greatest spaces. When by the grace of God man sees the glory of God, he sees him beyond the world of desire and then sorrows are left behind. (Mascaro, 1965, p. 90)

Here we see the idea of waking up to an unknown, interior truth, not accessible with the naked eye. The mystics of the Upanishads were discovering through their meditations and reflections, a pathway to enlightenment. By "constantly disciplining his senses, speaking the truth at all times, practicing non-violence, and behaving with detached equanimity to all" (Armstrong, 2006, p. 143), one came to know the Brahman, which was the Supreme Reality. It was a power higher, deeper, and more fundamental to existence. This power held the universe together and enabled all things to live. It could not be described or defined. It was all-encompassing. It was life itself and was best experienced in total silence. This was how one made contact with Brahman, or God.

The Upanishads are scriptures of the Indian mystics who had embarked on the path of inner peace. "The word "Upanishad" meant "to sit down near to"" (Armstrong, 2006, p. 150). The seeker was sitting near to God; the ineffable, inscrutable mystery of existence itself. It was a long and arduous journey to take.

The focus of the Upanishads was the atman, the self, which was identical with the brahman. If the sage could discover the inner heart of his own being, he would automatically enter into the ultimate reality and liberate himself from the terror of mortality. (Armstrong, 2006, pp. 148-149)

The way to the liberation was not easy. One must detach himself from his desires and live in a state of non-attachment. This is similar to what Christ said when he spoke 'Be in the world, but not of it'. One of the great mystic sages of the Upanishads was

Yajnavalkya. He "was convinced that there was, as it were, an immortal spark at the core of the human person, which participated in – was of the same nature as – the immortal brahman that sustained and gave life to the entire cosmos" (Armstrong, 2006, p. 151). God was an immanent presence and the ultimate reality of every human being. We could only discover this for ourselves by turning our attention inward. The atman, that which animated our personal existence and was intimately connected to Brahman or God, was the agent behind all of our senses, and even breathed us. Yajnavalkya explained:

You can't see the Seer who does the seeing; you can't hear the Hearer who does the hearing; you can't think with the Thinker who does the thinking; and you can't perceive the Perceiver who does the perceiving. The Self within the All [brahman] is this *atman* of yours. (Armstrong, 2006, pp. 151 – 153)

The Upanishads were designed to take us beyond the comprehension via the senses of the visible world and into the deeper layers of human consciousness. By plumbing the mysteries of our own nature, these mystics discovered we could transcend the world. What does this mean for us? When we expand our conscious awareness of who we really are at the deepest levels of existence, we expand consciousness itself. We gradually become aware of our immortal self, our soul, and our deeply personal connection to the impersonal force which governs all life in this universe, God, or as the mystics of the Upanishads called Him, Brahman. Brahman is consciousness. The more we experience this consciousness, the consciousness of God, the more aware we become of the consciousness of Oneness, a mystical truth of unity, sameness, and interconnectedness reflected in the mystical teaching of 'What is in one is in the Whole'. We can see this truth in our own lives: all human beings are designed the same; family instincts are identical across all cultures and civilizations; and that which makes us human, our humanitarian instincts are alike throughout the species. The next step is to recognize that when I do something wrong, it affects all of us (take a look at how much we are affected by the endless string of school shootings). We all suffer because of it. What is also true is the positive. When one of us does something good – a kindness, a service to others, or resisting the desire to respond to violence with an act of revenge and choose instead to respond with compassion – these acts benefit the whole, and teach what is possible when confronted with the darkness in others. As the experience of this becomes more frequent, we connect to that which is holy within ourselves; we are anchored in joy, peace, and contentment, and remain calm in spite of the storms around us; with continued practice of this inner journey into the realms of our own consciousness, we draw closer and closer to attaining the "bliss" of Brahman, of God.

UPANISHADS MEDITATION

I want you now to go deep within yourself, beyond the layers of the ego. Look at all your desires and attachments. See the things you cling to for your survival. Work; relationships; all the things we instinctively cling to. There's no judgment here. It's what we have conditioned ourselves to believe we must have in order to survive and live in this world. See them, thank them, and for the moment, let them go. See your attachments and desires dissolve away into nothingness. What freedom there is in this space! Dive deeper within. Connect to the animating agent that breathes you. That governs, regulates, and controls your inhale and exhale. Make contact with your Atman.

This inner core of your being is beyond thought, beyond feeling, beyond good and evil. Notice as you connect with it how calm, cool, patient, and collected you are. Seek your immortal Self that's not attached to this world. Who has no desires, fears, anxieties, or worries. Feel the bliss of this state begin to envelope you and release you from the endless cycles of suffering your soul has experienced. With the ecstatic knowledge of the Self, our Atman, we free ourselves from the endless desires and the ephemeral nature of the things here on earth. Life is an illusion that passes before our eyes. People come, people go. Once we identify with the Brahman, which contains the whole universe inside you, we are no longer on the wheels of suffering. The causes of our suffering are ignorance, egoism, aversion, attachment, and the desire to cling to life. Holding onto what is forever changing only adds to our suffering. When we let go of our ignorance (regarding the impermanent as permanent), our egoism (which believes we are the center of the universe instead of a part of the ineffable mystery; we identify our self with our ego and not our soul), our aversion (that which follows identification with painful experiences or memories; if we cannot avoid the things which produce unpleasant experiences, we suffer), our attachment (that which follows identification with pleasurable experiences or memories; if we cannot obtain what we desire, we inevitably suffer), and our desire to cling to life (the fear of death), we unlock the distortions of our minds and perceptions that prevent us from making contact with the Atman. When we gradually learn to consciously identify with the Atman, the Self, the Soul, the immortal spark within us, we come to know there is little to be gained by holding onto that which is limited.

We must not just understand this in metaphysical or spiritual terms. We must apply our understanding to our everyday life. Our actions in our life allow us to experience the Brahman. Treat people and all living things with kindness, compassion, and love. Do not do unto others what you would not have them do to you. All things share the same essence. All things share the same essence! When you understand this, your actions will follow in kind, good karma is attained, and one is then able to come to know and find one's Atman.

"The self that is free from evils, free from old age and death, free from sorrow, free from hunger and thirst, that is the self that you should try to discover" (Armstrong, 2006, p. 160).

Our goal is to look beyond the mind; beyond the body; beyond all our physical senses; and find the inner self that lives independently of all these functions.

When one says "I am speaking", it is the Spirit that speaks: the voice is the organ of speech. When one says "I am hearing", it is the Spirit that hears: the ear is the organ of hearing. And when one says "I think", it is the Spirit that thinks: the mind is the organ of thought. It is because of the light of the Spirit that the human mind can see, and can think, and enjoy this world. (Mascaro, 1965, p. 126)

In this space of perfect tranquility, serenity, and peace, having made contact with our Atman, let us sit quietly in silence and breathe in 5 long breaths.

And on your last breath, I want you to chant silently in your mind the sacred syllable "Om". This syllable stands for the very essence of the entire cosmos and unites us with it. "OM......"

Gently now, come back into the room, and when you are ready, open your eyes.

WORKBOOK QUESTIONS ON THE UPANISHADS

Both Gandhi and Martin Luther King Jr., believed in the principle of non-violence and taught this to their followers in seeking justice and liberation from their oppressors. Define the concept of *ahimsa* in your own words. Where does it apply in today's world? Are there situations where you find resistance in practicing *ahimsa*? Why?

These teachings grew out of a violent, aggressive world, much like the world we live in today. Are they still relevant, or do we need to find another way? Explain.

In your own words, define the Atman. Do you think this immortal part really exists?

Do all things share the same essence? Explain why or why not using evidence to support your claim.

BUDDHA AND THE PRACTICE OF MINDFULNESS

All life is *dukkha*. This is a central understanding at the core of almost all of the spiritual, mystical, and philosophical teachings that emerged from the Axial Age, this pivotal period in the history of humanity. *Dukkha* is a concept that all things are temporary; all states are temporary; and therefore, unsatisfying. It is often translated as "suffering" (Armstrong, 2006, p. 230). Experience of the physical world was conditioned by ignorance, sorrow, longing for what was, fear of the unknown, and the brief moments of life where we felt happiness. Yet, these "Moments of happiness were nearly always followed by periods of grief. Nothing lasted very long" (Armstrong, 2006, p. 230). People died; violence destroyed an individual's sense of peace, harmony, and justice and kept them in a perpetual state of fear and terror; illness, old age, and death were all that a person had to look forward to. Life was painful, unsatisfactory, and meaningless. It was pointless for people to attach themselves and cling to the ephemeral. What many of the Axial Age masters were seeking was a way for us to transcend our suffering and enter a state of liberation from the harsh reality of the temporal world. One of the greatest luminaries of the Axial Age, who not only reached liberation, but also exemplified what a human being could do and achieve, was the Buddha.

Buddha translates into the "awakened one" or the "enlightened one". Siddhartha Gautama breathed his first breath near the end of the 5th Century BCE. He was born in Lumbini (modern day Nepal) to King Suddhodana of the Shakya clan, and his wife Maya, the queen. Born into the warrior class, or the *Kshatriyas*, he was given the name Siddhartha, which means "he who achieves his aim" (http://www.biography.com/people/buddha-9230587). It was foretold by seers whom the king had called upon to examine his son and tell his fortune that Siddhartha would either be a great king or a great holy man. His father envisioned worldly ambitions for his son, and thus shielded him from the awareness of the grim cycles of suffering afflicting human life. King Suddhodana built a separate palace for his son, filled with luxury, opulence, and sensual pleasures. At 16 years old, Siddhartha married, and eventually had a son. All the worldly pleasures were at his feet. "Gotama's pleasure palace is a striking image of a mind in denial. As long as we persist in closing our hearts to the sorrow that surrounds us on all sides, we remain incapable of growth and insight" (Armstrong, 2006, p. 327).

When he was 29 years old, Siddhartha was restless, and decided to venture out beyond the palace to see his subjects. When he stepped outside the walls enclosing his pleasure sanctuary, he was shocked at the harsh realities of the human condition. He came across an old man; Siddhartha questioned his charioteer beside him who explained this was the fate of all people. He was deeply disturbed. Siddhartha ventured outside the palace more frequently, and on these succeeding visitations, he came face-to-face with a diseased man, a decaying corpse, and an ascetic. He learned the ascetic had renounced the world to seek an end to his personal suffering and fear of death. Amid all the disease and disintegration of life, the monk had found a way to remain calm and serene. So overcome by all that he had seen outside the walls,

Siddhartha renounced his life of pleasures and opulence, for he had now recognized happiness in the physical world was transitory. He left his kingdom, wife, and son to find a way to release humanity from *dukkha* – from universal suffering, aging, sickness, and death. As with Siddhartha, we can see ourselves in the same light. "Once the suffering that is an inescapable part of the human condition has broken through the cautionary barricades that we have erected against it, we can never see the world in the same way again" (Armstrong, 2006, p. 328).

Gautama was seeking the blissful state of liberation called *nirvana*, which translates from the Sanskrit as a "blowing out" (Armstrong, 2006, pp. 326 – 327). The idea behind this is by extinguishing the self, the ego, and all the passions and desires that locked him to the conditional, corrupted, and ephemeral world, all pain and suffering would be transcended; one could then exist in the unborn, ageless, incorruptible, and griefless state of our true existence. The quest was for a fully awakened consciousness within the individual that transcended his mortal limitations in the physical world and would unite him with the true reality of the cosmos. Siddhartha sought out a spiritual teacher. For 6 years Siddhartha lived an ascetic life, studied and mastered two different forms of meditation practiced in India at that time, and quickly ascended to teacher, "but ultimately he found that the techniques did not produce the state of complete freedom from desire that he sought" (Myss, 2003, p. 99). Determined to find a path to enlightenment, Siddhartha endeavored to study yogic practices, pranayama or breath control, and even self-mortification. He abstained from eating food for weeks at a time, but this only weakened his body and left him frail. "Finally he reached the conclusion that extremes of self-denial would eventually end in death and a resumption of the endless wheel of *samsara* – birth, death, and rebirth" (Myss, 2003, p.99). Exhausted, Siddhartha recalled a time when he had experienced total tranquility watching his father plow a field as a child. He remembered he had sat under a tree while watching and was free of all desires and cravings. A childhood memory of complete "bliss" guided Siddhartha to sit under the Bodi Tree, which is now known as the tree of enlightenment. Later, after his enlightenment and when he began his teachings, Gautama Buddha would exhort his followers not to blindly follow anyone's teachings, no matter how venerable they may be, "if those teachings did not tally with their own experience" (Armstrong, 2006, p. 329). The Buddha wanted you to find *nirvana* for yourselves, and that you, and only you, can do it. "No one saves us but ourselves. No one can and no one may. We ourselves must walk the path" (http://www.brainy-quote.com/quotes/quotes/b/buddha385920.html).

After pushing himself to extreme austerity in the ascetic life, Gautama came to the conclusion that his extremism was not helping him to achieve his spiritual quest. He realized a path of balance was the appropriate path to follow and he would call this "The Middle Way." While contemplating the Middle Way, Siddhartha sat under the Bodhi Tree and vowed not to leave until he had found the answer to the question he was seeking which was how to end human suffering. "Plunging himself into deep meditation, by nightfall he had entered into a superconscious state of illumination that is said to have lasted forty-nine days" (Myss, 2003, p.100). While sitting there for all those days, he continuously emptied and purified his mind, and battled with both inner and outer demons. He was tempted by Mara (which translates as "Death", the Evil One) with various spectacles – fears, intimidations, compulsions, and when that didn't work, temptation. Impervious to the seductions of the Evil One, Mara and his demons withdrew. Siddhartha had discovered the state of being for which he had been seeking. The truths to the questions of how to end humanity's suffering finally came, and in that moment, he attained pure enlightenment. Henceforward, he would be known as The Buddha, or "he who is awake" (http://www.biography.com/people/buddha-9230587).

The Buddha practiced a form of mindfulness in which

he scrutinized his behavior at every moment of the day, noting the ebb and flow of feelings and sensations, together with the fluctuations of his consciousness, and making himself aware of the constant stream of desires, irritations, and ideas that coursed through his mind in the space of a single hour. (Armstrong, 2006, p. 330)

The reason he did this was to become acquainted with how his own mind worked, how his body worked, so that he could learn how to master himself. He observed that it wasn't just old age, sickness, and death that caused suffering; but also pain, grief, despair, anger, apathy, being close to what we hate or distant from one we love, or not getting what we want. He observed how one craving led to another, and how he was never satisfied with who he was. There was this constant yearning inside of him to do something, become something, and get something he felt he needed. This restlessness of the mind and body led to suffering, and in this world predicated on change, if we were caught in this endless cycle of desires, our suffering would never end.

At the same time he contemplated the negative truths about life, the Buddha fostered a mindfulness practice to free himself from hatred, pain, grief, anger, and suffering by infusing his mind with thoughts "full of compassion, desiring the welfare of all living beings" (Armstrong, 2006, p. 331). He systematically banished one thought after the other, and the more he did this, the calmer his mind became. With consistency, discipline, and determination, mindfulness would transform an individual away from the cravings, desires, and selfishness of the ego and lift the aspirant to acquire a level of compassion that connected him to his humanity. These meditations were called "the immeasurables" (Armstrong, 2006, p. 332), and were designed to open up the individual to his whole being and to tear down the barriers that separated him from others. If we could learn how to transcend our egos, extend benevolence to all human beings and creatures, direct our intention to all corners of the world and engage in the undifferentiated expression of unconditional love, our minds would eventually break free from its self-preoccupation, and feel "expansive, without limits, enhanced, without hatred or petty malevolence" (Armstrong, 2006, p. 332). This was how an individual could achieve *nirvana*. It wasn't something that would happen overnight; in fact, it would take many, many years, perhaps a lifetime to reach *nirvana*, but with skill, discipline, dedication and practice, mindfulness achieved this by slow degrees. Enlightenment and the ultimate truth of reality, as the Buddha discovered, come to us when we commit ourselves to going all the way on our spiritual journeys.

"THE IMMEASURABLE" MEDITATION

"Do not dwell in the past, do not dream of the future, concentrate the mind on the present moment" (http://www.brainyquote.com/quotes/quotes/b/buddha101052). Breathe in the timeless presence of this eternal moment. Eternity is not found anywhere else but in the now; an ever expanding series of 'nows' which you are a part of. Breathe in the magnificence of who you are. You're not your thoughts, you're not your feelings or emotions, you're not your past, and you're not your future. Let all things fall by the wayside. Our sufferings, your suffering is caused by your desires, your attachments, and your longings for things to be different than what they are. For just a brief moment, in this moment, give yourself permission to be free of all that causes you to suffer. All the pains, traumas, disappointments, frustrations, loneliness, anger, violence done to you, or that you may have done to others, your grief, your despair, your fears of old age, sickness, and death. In this moment, let it go. Allow yourself to be consciously aware of the conscious awareness surrounding you. Dive deep into this awareness, this consciousness, that is the birthplace of your own consciousness and awareness. It is ineffable, unchangeable, forever still and calm, deathless, taintless, and independent. This is "the Truth", "the Subtle", "the Everlasting". Peace, purity, freedom, safety, and incomprehensible serenity are its attributes. Allow yourself to touch this place that exists within you. This is your safe haven, your oasis of calm. Breathe this in deeply.

In this state of profound serenity, let us cultivate an attitude of friendship for everything and every human being. See in your mind's eye both friend and foe. And extend sympathy of loving-kindness to both. Allow yourself to feel the love you have for your brother and sister, offer them love, and now see your enemy, and extend it to him or her as well. At the ultimate reality of existence, there is no difference regardless of what the personality of the egos may be. Be friend to all in this moment. Recognize the Oneness of life.

Next, let us choose a person who is suffering. A homeless child; a veteran on the streets; a person with cancer; someone who has lost their beloved; someone with depression; the lonely; the crippled. Choose one and empathize with their pain. Feel what it is they are suffering from. Feel their anger, fear, rejection, depression, and terror. Through your empathizing with their suffering, feel how natural it is to feel compassion for them. Let this feeling of compassion fill you up as you bless this human being with thoughts of loving-kindness.

As we draw our attention away from this person, let us summon up an image of joy that delights our souls. Maybe it's the sight of children playing; lovers embracing; laughing with friends; a marriage; going to a ball game; sitting with the family on the porch after a Sunday meal. Whatever it is, I want you to delight in the joy of others, without any feelings of envy, jealousy, hate, or resentment. Joy is our natural state. See this joyous image in your mind's eye, be happy for those who are experiencing this joy, and notice how this joy fills you up too. Don't allow anything to interfere with the sympathetic joy you feel seeing other people's happiness. See their happiness as a reflection of your own joy and happiness for your life. Breathe in. Breathe out.

Finally, let us open ourselves to the wholeness and well-being of all who live on our planet. See in your mind's eye the whole earth, our beautiful blue planet, our home. Extend thoughts of loving-kindness to every single living thing. Say these thoughts silently to yourselves as you extend it to all life forms: "May you be well. May you be free of pain and suffering. May you be whole."

In this space of loving-kindness and compassion for the whole world, let us breathe in silence 5 long, slow breaths.

And on your last breath, as you start to come back into the room, I want to leave you with these words from the Buddha:

You can search throughout the entire universe for someone who is more deserving of your love and affection than you are yourself, and that person is not to be found anywhere. You yourself, as much as anybody in the entire universe deserve your love and affection. (http://www.brainyquote.com/quotes/quotes/b/buddha132910.html)

Gently now, come back into the room, and when you are ready, open your eyes.

WORKBOOK QUESTIONS ON THE BUDDHA AND MINDFULNESS

Practice the Buddha's mindfulness. Take a minute and search what's going on with you. Note your feelings, sensations, thoughts, desires, frustrations, etc., and write them down. What would life be like if you didn't have all this stuff clouding your mind?

What is consciousness?

Name some of the barriers you've erected to keep you separated from others. How are they serving you? What could you do to start tearing these walls down that keep you from transcending your ego?

Do you believe it is possible for you to achieve enlightenment? Why or why not?

What is your most treasured lesson from this book?

BIBLIOGRAPHY

Armstrong, K. (2006). *The Great Transformation: The Beginning of Our Religious Traditions.*

New York: Anchor Books.

Buddha. (n.d.). BrainyQuote.com. Retrieved December 8, 2015, from BrainyQuote.com Web

Site: http://www.brainyquote.com/quotes/quotes/b/buddha385920.html

Buddha. (n.d.). BrainyQuote.com. Retrieved December 8, 2015, from BrainyQuote.com Web

Site: http://www.brainyquote.com/quotes/quotes/b/buddha101052

Buddha. (n.d.). BrainyQuote.com. Retrieved December 8, 2015, from BrainyQuote.com Web

Site: http://www.brainyquote.com/quotes/quotes/b/buddha132910.html

Buddha Biography. (n.d.). Retrieved December 7, 2015, from the Biography.com Web site:

http://www.biography.com/people/buddha-9230587

Carl Jung. (n.d.). BrainyQuotes.com. Retrieved December 5, 2015, from BrainyQuotes.com Web

Site: http://www.brainyquote.com/quotes/quotes/c/carl-jung132738.html

Eliade, M. (1958). *Rites and Symbols of Initiation: The Mysteries of Birth and Rebirth.* (W. R.

Trask, Trans.). New York: Harper & Row Publishers.

Gyatso,G.K. (n.d.). AboutBuddha.org. Retrieved December 7, 2015, from AboutBuddha.org

Web site: http://www.aboutbuddha.org/english/life-of-buddha.htm/

Hamilton, E., & Cairns, H. (Eds.). (1989). *Plato: The Collected Dialogues.* Princeton, NJ:

Princeton University Press.

Holy Bible, King James Version. (2014). Nashville, TN: Holman Bible Publishers.

Lao Tzu. (n.d.). BrainyQuote.com. Retrieved December 7, 2015, from BrainyQuote.com Web

Site: http://www.brainyquote.com/quotes/quotes/l/laotzu393061.html

Lao Tzu. (n.d.). GoodReads.com. Retrieved December 7, 2015, from GoodReads.com Web Site:

http://www.goodreads.com/quotes/341604-do-you-have-the-patience-to-wait-till-your-mud

Lao Tzu. (n.d.). GoodReads.com. Retrieved December 7, 2015, from GoodReads.com Web Site:

http://www.goodreads.com/
quotes/125184-if-there-is-to-be-peace-in-the-world-there

Lao Tzu Biography. (n.d.). Retrieved December 6, 2015, from
Encyclopedia of World Biography

Web site: http://www.notablebiographies.com/Ki-Lo/Lao-Tzu.html

Littlejohn, R. (n.d.). *Laozi (Lao Tzu, fl. 6th cn. B.C.E)*. Retrieved
December 6, 2015, from

Internet Encyclopedia of Philosophy Web Site: http://www.iep.
utm.edu/laozi/#H4

Mascaro, J. (1965). *The Upanishads*. New York: Penguin Books.

Myss, C. (2003). *Sacred Contracts: Awakening Your Divine
Potential*. New York: Harmony Books.

Shay, J.S. (1994). *Achilles in Vietnam*. New York: Scribner.

Tao Te Ching. (2006). Retrieved December 6, 2015, from www.
Taoism.net and *Tao Te Ching:*

Annotated & Explained, published by SkyLight Paths: http://www.
Taoism.net/ttc/complete.htm

Tick, E. (2005). *War and the Soul*. Wheaton, Il: Quest Books.

Violatti, C. (2013). Siddhartha Gautama. In *Ancient History
Encyclopedia*, last modified

December 9, 2013. Retrieved December 7, 2015, from Ancient.eu
Web site: http://www.ancient.eu/Siddhartha_Gautama/